T0106726

Keeping It Real

Keeping It Real

Through the Storm

Amanda M. Dixon

KEEPING IT REAL
THROUGH THE STORM

Scripture quotations from the Holy Bible, King James Version (Authorized Version). First published in 1611. Quoted from the KJV Classic Reference Bible.

Scripture quotations marked NIV are taken from the Holy Bible, New International Version®. NIV®. Copyright © 1973, 1978, 1984 by International Bible Society. Used by permission of Zondervan. All rights reserved. [Biblica]

iUniverse books may be ordered through booksellers or by contacting:

iUniverse
1663 Liberty Drive
Bloomington, IN 47403
www.iuniverse.com
1-800-Authors (1-800-288-4677)

ISBN: 978-1-5320-4646-9 (sc)
ISBN: 978-1-5320-4647-6 (e)

Library of Congress Control Number: 2018903814

Print information available on the last page.

iUniverse rev. date: 04/12/2018

Contents

About the Book

I HAVE WRITTEN THIS BOOK as a way to talk about things that happen in everyday life. In the book I discuss many topics on life in general and the many struggles people face. I talk about some personal experiences in life and things I have faced. The book explains some ways to overcome problems, situations, circumstances and personal life challenges. I clearly speak about things such as relationships problems and what cause them, emotional trauma, struggling, teenage pregnancy, forgiveness, trust, focusing on one's own life, and much more. I also pinpoint certain insecurities people suffer from and how they might be able to overcome them. Some of the Content is followed by scriptures from the King James Version of the Holy Bible. I also wrote the book titled (Keeping it Real the Reality of it All} that was published in the year 2007.

Choose Your Battles

MOST OF THE CHOICES WE make in life are totally up to us. We have a lot of options to discover our own destiny. Sometimes we make choices in life that we later find out are not the best choices. We have freedom to pick and choose who we want in our lives and what kind of future to look forward to. We have the right to set our own goals in life and all opportunity to carry them out. We are free to have our own expectations from other people, places, and things. Although we choose the wrong way to go at times, it is up to us to pick up the pieces and journey on. No one can make up our mind for us. God gives us each a mind of our own. We must use it wisely because if we make the wrong decisions, "we will later suffer the consequences."

If you want to live a good, healthy, prosperous, productive life, you must choose positive people to be around who are on the same level, and are beneficial to you physically, mentally, emotionally, and in some cases financially. Choose people who are suitable for the life you want to live. If you want to live a happy life, choose to be around people who will bring you joy and happiness. Be around people who are full of great intentions. Don't deal with people who don't care about life, what it has to offer and who will suck the life right out of you. Make sure you are among people who are on your level of success. Always be mindful of your surroundings. If you want the finer things in life then you must work hard to achieve them. "If a man does not work he does not eat." Things don't always work the way we want them to in life but we have alternate ways of making them better. If we want success then we must choose the right career path and follow our dreams. "All things are possible through Christ who strengthens us."

We pick and choose our own battles. If you are heading down a productive path and hang with the wrong crowd, chances are that they will try to bring you down with them. Some people don't pull you down intentionally, but they just don't see life as you see it and can care less how your life turns out. It is very sad to say but it is ever so true. We must use time wisely and not waists time on people, places and things that have no sense of purpose or motivation in life. We can't get time back that we waist on others and we will find people that will waist our precious time. Time is priceless and it has value.

Why put yourself in a situation that you will later regret? If you find yourself doing something that is going to cost you everything that you have worked hard for, cut the cords, you have all opportunity to walk away without looking back. You must know to never stay in a situation that is just messy. Once you accept a battle you have to fight it and if you are not properly geared up with the word of God, you better believe it is going to be a tough one. Yes God sees us through all of our battles but he gives us the choice to not encounter them. We fall down and we get back up but what do we do to prevent ourselves from falling in the first place? God gives His toughest battles to his strongest soldiers.

Author Experience

We all want the best things in life and most of the time we are knowledgeable of the things we need to do in order to achieve them. I always dreamed of going to school and getting some kind of degree so that I could have a great job. I wanted to be able to take care of my own family when I got one. I always dreamed of falling in love one day and marrying the man of my dreams. I wanted whoever it was to have the dame intentions that I had in life. "He would be someone who would work as hard as I did or maybe harder." Let's be honest and keep it real, how many people can honestly say that they never had dreams in life that didn't turn out according to plan? I know I am not the only one.

Unfortunately my life didn't turn out according to my plans. I invested sixteen years of my life into a relationship that was not so healthy or prosperous. There was no spiritual connection, or financial growth. Although people say you have to make things work, Sometime's you have to realize that you cannot change a person if they are not willing to change for him or herself. I held on for as long as I could. Let's just say that I had to walk away in order to discover myself.

People of God know that we are all going to face some kind of battles in life. We must know the strength god gives us to endure until the end but we must also be wise and know when the battle is over. Be conscious in knowing when time is winding down. If you are not happy in life and everything is a constant battle, realize it is time to walk away. Realize when you have chosen the wrong battle. Even though we are told to never give up and throw in the towel, God will let us know when enough is enough.

(POEM)

One Day at a Time

THE GOOD THE BAD, INDIFFERENT is what we have to take one day at a time. The chaos the pointless drama the endless situations and circumstances we have to take them one day at a time, the hurt pain the frustration and disappointment just one day at a time. The thoughtfulness the thoughtlessness the troublesome times take them one day at a time. The sickness, weakness, the heartbreak is what we take in but take it one day at a time. The struggles, breakdowns, breakups and the sleepless nights take them just one day at a time. The confusion, criticism, unexpected downfalls, the highs the lows, the crying the sighing, is what we encounter but take it one day at a time. The lying the dyeing the cheating the death and destruction no one wants to endure so we cover it up by silence and the act of denying but it takes one day at a time. The uncertainty the disbelief the moments of despair and the grinding of our teeth don't fall for it live with it and try to get through it. Take it one day at a time. Life can be a handful life can be a mess it can have you over the top or on the edge life can leave you torn up on the inside feeling alone and ready to die. Don't take it for granted and don't let it pass you by just live it, love it, embrace it and take it one day at a time.

Change

DON'T EVER JUDGE YOURSELF TO someone else's standards. God made you who you are for a reason. Don't ever let anyone pull you out of your character. Some people will try to belittle you just to make you feel less than what you are worth and make you feel some type of way like you have done something wrong. They do it in an attempt to turn you from the greatness inside of you to bring you to their level. They want you to downsize your standards to their way of living or thinking. God has created in you a character full of integrity, and the enemy is trying to sift you as wheat. "He is trying to devour you and turn you into something you are not." Be steadfast and unmovable, do those things that are pleasing in God's sight, in spite of the adversary.

One of the biggest problems in the world today is that people are afraid of change. They are busy listening to reason when they should be focusing on their walk with the Master and creator of all things. Without God we would have nothing or be nothing. If you know a person has no Godly intentions or desire to walk right before Christ, you should not by any means think that you can change them. Change first comes from within oneself. If a person is not willing to make sacrifices and steps towards living right, "what makes you think you can change their perspective? There is nothing you can say or do "other than pray" to make them see things different. They have to have a made up mind to want to change. They have to want change as much as you want them to change. Everyone had to learn to walk as a child and so it is when life progresses into adulthood. You have to embrace, want, and accept change when you decide to walk for Christ. As long as a person does their part, God will begin to mold them into the being they are trying to become. Only God can change someone Him and Him alone. Individuals have to put forth all efforts and believe in their hard of hearts that change will come. Faith without work is dead.

1st John 5:4 For whatsoever is born of God over cometh the world: and this is the victory that over cometh the world, even our faith. (King James Bible on Line- 1st John 5:4)

Author Experience

A prophet once told me that just because you have children by someone doesn't mean you have to marry them nor can you change them. You don't have to stay with them for the rest of your life. He was basically letting me know that God has someone for everyone and the person who I was with was not the one. He was not the Chosen one from God. He was not the man God intended for me to marry. God knew what kind of character and integrity was built inside of me and He was trying to protect my heart. I was not to spend a portion of my life in misery. "It was warning before destruction." How many know we sometimes don't want to listen to reason we would rather learn the hard way? I thought as long as I was living right or trying to live right that the other person would change his ways. I didn't realize that I was in for a rude awakening. "Never second guess God's plans. I started encountering more problems than I had ever imagined. "If I would have only listened to the voice of God my life would have been much greater." The moment I said I do I started encountering more problems than a little bit.

I was lied to cheated on, disrespected, used abused, and the list goes on. I began to question God as if it were His fault. I say all this to say, young ladies you don't have to be no mans security blanket, easy access or hand maid to make him change and to make him love you. The bible clearly tells us that He who finds a wife finds a good thing. "You should never settle for less than who God says you are or who he wants you to be with." God crested in you a woman full or great character, integrity, power, success and He wants' to give you much more. You cannot change someone who does not have all or most of these qualifications. The Lord of Hosts wants to give you Joy and peace that surpassed all understanding. He wants to fill your heart with joy and contentment and cannot do anything if you are trying to change someone who is not willing to be your backbone or source of strength. Have faith in God and trust His plans. He cannot work if you are busy trying to change what is meant to destroy you. Do right by people and demand the same respect. "Follow your dreams." God gives us power over the enemy and he will give you strength to carry on in spite of what things look like.

Isaiah 40:29 He giveth power to the faint; and to them that have no might increaseth strength. (King James Bible on Line-Isaiah 40:29)

Life Has Meaning after the Storm

SOMETIMES IT'S HARD TO SEE the clear picture because your mind is entangled in what you have been through. "It's very hard to realize that there is more to life, when you have been through so much." It is almost impossible or difficult to see that there is more to life than meets the eye. When you are bound by things that happen to you in life you begin to believe that there is no hope. You have lost all hope. It is hard to see that life can and will be what you hoped and dreamed for. There comes a point in life that you have to stop, focus and understand that the things you went through were temporary. "You can and will be who God says you are and wants you to be. Believe in yourself and focus on what makes you happy. Gain control of yourself and walk in contentment. Sometimes we get stuck in what people call a comfort zone. If we spend more time praying, fasting, and seeking guidance, God is able to pull us out of that comfort zone. He will remove people places and things that are toxic to our wellbeing. He will protect us from all hurt, harm and danger. He will give us resources that will help us build confidence and persevere.

Realize that no matter what the situation or circumstances, everyone has been through something. While you wonder and anticipate you story's ending, someone else's story is just beginning. No one can tell your story like you can. Although you have had bad experiences in life, your story does not end there. Know that other people have experienced something far worse. When you think you are telling people your life story, you can actually help someone overcome some things that might have them bound or trapped.

Although life brings many challenges and disappointments we must not waddle in regret. We must know that life has meaning before, during, and after the storm. There is still life after every test and trial. Some people lose hope and refuse to believe in life after a storm. Their minds are wounded, confused and it's hard for them to see the clearer picture. They see no light at the end of the tunnel. Everyone faces some kind of storm or test in life be it big or small, a storm is a storm. There are many types of storms in life but if you go through knowing, trusting and believing that life still has meaning, you will conquer all your fears.

Storms are meant to break us but they make us strong. Although we find that hard to believe, we must know that beyond the shadow of a doubt that our God reigns over the just as well as the unjust. When we are faced with difficult storms and the storms of life are raging, we must push and pray harder than ever. We must seek guidance get a clear understanding and use wisdom and knowledge. Knowledge is power so let non storm hold you to a point that you fall short of God's glory. We fall short but with grace and mercy, we are able to withstand the tests if times.

Forgiveness

FORGIVENESS IS A VIRTUE. LIFE has its way
of knocking us down by people we love and trust the most but we
must learn to forgive them. Yes it is easier said than done but in
due time we have to forgive those people who have tremendously
caused us pain and internal damage. We have to forgive the ones
who might have us to a point of no return and caused us to lose
focus on who we really are. "We have to forgive those who have
stolen from us, lied to us, cheated, raped, or molested us. As hard
as it is or may seem we have to forgive these sick minded beasts.
Even though these are people we wish would never see the light
of day again or walk earth no longer, we must learn the meaning
of forgiveness. It's hard to rest easy at night knowing that someone
has inflicted pain or critically wounded us and we have to forgive
them. How do we forgive people that have destroyed our inner
being and the pain will won't go away? That is a question that is
hard for anyone to answer.

Even though that person who has hurt you should come and
beg your forgiveness, sometimes we have to take initiative and go
to that individual, remind them of the damage they have caused
and tell them that we forgive them. You have to approach that
person whole heartedly and say no matter the circumstances, "I
forgive you for what you have done to me. If your heart is not in,
it than it is not sincere, will it take the pain away? No it will not

only time can heal those open wounds. When you harm another human being even though it seems to others as it does not bother you, deep down inside it really does. You have to attempt to approach that human being and let them know that you are sorry for what you did and you beg their forgiveness. You have to ask them to pardon your wrong doings. This will lift some weight off of you and in some cases it will lift some stuff off the person you hurt. You must know that all though the odds are against you, you have taken the first step towards your free will to live.

Have you ever been in a situation where you know you have hurt someone or did something wrong and don't know how to approach the person? This happens when people are unsure of the outcome and afraid of consequences. People are afraid of the other person rejecting their forgiveness. Sometimes it is hard due to shame or guilt. When you ask for forgiveness whole heartedly, you must then put it in God's hands. He will deal with it in due time according to the situation. You must then repent. Have you ever been in a situation where someone hurt you and you were waiting for them to apologize? You cannot make someone apologize. If their heart and mind convicts them of their wrong doing, they will eventually come to you. It is in that moment when you have to decide if their apology is genuine. We are all human and we all make mistakes. The only one that needs to understand and overcome the situation is the parties involved. Only God can fix the situation or circumstances.

Author Experience

After the raw deals and endless pain life has dealt me, I carried hatred in my heart towards people for a long period of time. How many are guilty of this? I didn't think that I should have to forgive and I didn't want to forgive the people that hurt me the most. I actually contemplated ways of seeking revenge on everyone who had ever hurt me. I wanted them to hurt and suffer the same way I was hurting. I wanted them to feel my pain. I felt like they should experience something to make them hurt. I had to pray and ask God to help me cope with the art of forgiveness as I dealt with my uncontrolled emotions. I asked to him to create in me a clean unforgiving heart.

Mark 3:29 But he that shall blaspheme against the Holy Ghost hath never forgiveness, but is in danger of eternal damnation: because they said, He hath an unclean spirit. (King James Bible on Line-Mark 3:29)

Genesis 27:45 until thy brothers anger turn away from thee, and he forget that which thou hast done to him: then will I send, and fetch thee from thence: why should I be deprives also of you both in one day? (King James Bible on Line-Genesis 27:45)

Job 9:27 If I say, I will forget my complaint, I will leave off my happiness, and comfort myself. (King James Bible on Line-Job 9:27)

Job 11:16 Because thou shalt forget thy misery, and remember it as waters that pass away. (King James Bible on Line-Job 11:16)

Respect- A feeling of deep admiration for someone or something elicited by their abilities, qualities, or achievements.

The respect levels in this world we live in today are so low it's not even funny. A lot of young people don't have respect for parents, elders, or no one in authority figure. It is so different from the way I was taught when I was growing up. Men don't respect women. Women don't respect men. Children don't respect their parents, and so on and so forth. When I was a child growing up, children were not allowed in the same room with a bunch of adults that were in a conversation. They were not allowed to participate in the conversation of adults. We often wonder why some children don't understand the meaning of respect. Not to say all children, because some children have a lot of respect for adults or authority figure. In some cases children are taught and some just don't care or listen.

We must realize that in order to gain respect, you must give respect. Sometimes we have to be mindful of the things we say or do in front of others to gain their respect. People tend to repeat or do what they say or hear. No matter how often they are told not to they do it anyway. We always desire respect not realizing the things we have to do to earn it. Sometimes the same respect we dish out will be the same we get in return. Not only do respect need to be implemented in children, parents, and families. It has to be give and take on jobs, in schools, and in communities as a whole. We have to learn to respect people's positions. When you are on a job you have to respect your boss, supervisor, or co-workers. They have to return that same respect. People need to set accept and respect boundaries. Who can honestly say that they have been disrespectful to someone in any way? Who can honestly say that they have been disrespectful at some point?

I'll be the first to admit that I have felt disrespected numerous times in my life. I may have even been disrespectful to some people. Some may have deserved it and maybe some didn't. When you have been disrespected it gives you an outlook on life and makes you wonder if you deserved it. When you disrespect people in life you have to pause and ask yourself if that person deserved it. Realistically speaking, no one deserves to be disrespected in any way, shape, form or fashion. Respect is a two way street. It is earned not rewarded.

(POEM)

Time Waits for no One

You can't erase time and you can't get it back.
No one can buy time because time is precious and priceless.
Don't waste time on senseless people places or things that
Have no meaning. Use time wisely and appreciate the
Time people invest in you. You can't wait for or anticipate
time. You can't rewind time or get time back. Time is of value
time can be fun but remember that time waits for no one.

Domestic Violence- Abuse, battering, or family violence, a
pattern of behavior which involves violence or other abuse by one
person against another in a domestic setting such as a marriage
or cohabitation, violent or aggressive behavior within the home,
typically the violent abuse of a spouse or partner. (Google)

Somehow today's cold, crucial world we live in is full of people
that have grasped a concept of thinking it is okay to be physically
abusive to others. Not in any way should an individual build up so
much anger inside of them that take it out on someone by putting
their hands on them. Domestic violence has a percentage in deaths
today. (Google) Nearly one out of four women has experienced
violence by a spouse or boyfriend. (Google) Approximately

seven million children live in families in which severe partner violence occurred. (Google) Many families are broken up and seriously affected as a result of domestic violence. (Google) A lot of domestic violence stems from heated arguments over money or finances, jealousy, or insecurities. In some cases the parties involved realize that these things could have been prevented with more communication. (Google)

Why do people feel they have the right to physically abuse others? Just because you are in a relationship with someone does not give you the right to put your hands on them. No matter how bad things may seem, or how complicated a situation gets no one should build up enough anger to strike or hit someone they claim to love or have feelings for. Although people cannot handle so many mixed emotions, they should not let it cause them to start hitting, fighting, or physically abusing anyone in any way. It is no secret that a lot of domestic violence cases resorts to murder or suicide. Men Abuse women and women abuse men. When did it become ok to beat up on people and use them for punching bags or a way to relieve stress? "It is not ok." If you love someone you should not want to cause them physical harm at all. God did not create unions for people to hurt each other. He created them for the sake of love.

Children who grow up around domestic violence sometimes don't even want to be in relationships. Some end up in abusive relationships because they think it is ok. Some grow up afraid to trust people. Some just repeat the same life style because that's all they know. Some people have to seek counseling or other types of therapy after being physically or mentally abused by someone they thought loved and cared about them. Some people become traumatized just by witnessing abuse. Young men grow up thinking it is ok to beat up on women because they watched daddy do it to mommy all their lives. Young ladies think it is ok because mommy tolerated all the time.

Domestic violence is not healthy for any relationship or

marriage. When you are in a relationship and every argument turns into a physical altercation, it is time to seek some professional help or simply walk away and break all ties. Why live in misery? If two individuals can't agree to disagree on anything at all, they are not happy ant it will cause more harm. If you are in a relationship and feel as if the only way to get a point across or prove something is to hit someone then you need serious help. Jails are over populated and a percentage of them are males serving time for domestic violence charges. Some of them are even facing life sentences for murder.

Honesty

HONESTY IS ONE OF THE best qualities a person can possess in life. If you cannot be honest with yourself first, how can you be honest with other people? No one wants to admit any faults or wrong doings in life but who are we kidding, and who wants to be lied to? You have to obtain an honest attitude in every aspect of life. Some people always expect honest answers but wouldn't know how to tell the truth if it slapped them in the face. Honesty is the back bone to building great character and it causes people to trust you more. When you can trust people or people can trust you, they begin to believe in you and they will always accept and respect your intentions. When you are not honest with people and always lie, it creates trust issues. People will not believe anything you say or do. If you constantly lie and deceive people you are not an honest individual. "People honor and admire honesty." People will never respect a liar.

If lying is a way to get you out of every situation, you need to change your way of thinking. There will come a point that people who are not honest will be telling the truth and because of their history, no one will believe them. If you have great intentions in life and want to make the best of every situation, always be honest with yourself and other people. Do everything in decency, hear the truth, speak the truth, listen to the truth, live the truth, be the truth, and walk in the truth. A lot of people miss out on blessings because they are never completely honest. Although it may seem hard at times, always hold tight to your integrity. Even if people are not completely honest with you still remain honest and straight forward. "Always tell the truth even when it might hurt someone. The truth hurts but it will set you free from worry and bondage. Not being honest created the majority of problems in relationships, marriages, businesses and friendships.

In this world we live in today no one wants to hear the truth because it steps on a lot of toes. If ninety percent of the world would tell the truth and be honest with people then this world would not have so many problems. The world suffers from lack of communication and understanding due to people being so dishonest. How many people can say that there has never been a time in their life that they were not completely honest about something? Some people have to learn not to be blind to the truth because there are people out there who know how to dress up lies and deception very well. I can honestly say that although life has thrown me a lot of lemons, I always try to maintain my integrity. Although life has its way of disappointing you with lies and deception, "always remember that being honest will carry you far in life."(Author)

Focus

PART OF THE REASON WHY people can't see past their own faults is because they are always worried about the lives of others. If at least half of the world would focus on their relationships with family, friends and their own relationships, or their futures then this world would be a better place. People would prosper more if they focus on self. No one wants to admit that at some point in life they lost focus on what they were doing because something or someone else caught their attention. The truth remains that most have been guilty of this, because no one is perfect. We all have faults and imperfections. In today's society every thought counts for something. Just because you see people doing well or living good and having a great time, does not mean that life has always been a walk in the park for them. Everything is not always peaches and cream.

Everyone has to start somewhere to get to where they are going or want to be in life. God gives us all a measure of faith. If you put your faith to work and believe in your hopes and dreams then you won't waste time focusing on others. Some people start from bottom to get to the top while others start at the top and hit rock bottom. A prime example of this is when you see someone driving a nice car, you will assume they have a lot of money but you don't know what they went through to get that car. Another example is maybe you see a homeless man on the street and assume he needs to get a job or he doesn't care about life but you don't know where he was before he became homeless. You never know a person's situation or what predicament they might have been in.

Sometimes we wonder why people take time and attention away from their own surroundings to pay attention to the surroundings of other's. It is simply the lack of faith they have. It is the uncertainty that they have what it takes to be just as prosperous as the next person. Prosperity begins with focusing on one's own life. If we take time to focus on our goals then we will know and understand what we need to conquer our fears and overcome doubt. Then our hopes and dreams will come alive. If we don't lose focus we will be able to fulfill the plan and purpose God has for us, and we will reach our destiny.

People are too busy focusing on and being jealous of what others have and trying to do what other people do. They are busy doing what it takes to become someone else. Never sell yourself short of your own success because you would rather focus and be like someone else. Instead set goals in your life and stay focused. Be so focused that nothing or no one can distract you from achieving anything you put your mind to. Pray for all things, through every situation, and believe in your prayers as well as believing in yourself. Keep the lords commandments.

(POEM)

Contentment

I'M SO GLAD TROUBLES DON'T last always. Grateful that God gives purpose to a new day. Happy that yesterday is gone and all my sins' are washed away. I know tomorrow wasn't promised but I made it so I'm on my way to see if people listen to what I have to say. I will tell my story of how I did it for His glory. I made it through the night without a fight and woke up to the brightness of daylight. I'll tell the world how I thought it was over but I'm still here even though I thought no one cared of the weight I bared. I didn't think God would forgive the life that I lived but I prayed and believed and He really did so ill shine my light to the darkness of night. Sometimes people need to know that it takes time to grow. He walked me through and He will walk with you too if you pray and believe His blessings you will receive. You don't have to yell but don't be afraid to tell of how He brought you out without a doubt and there's no more resentment because you walk in contentment.

(POEM)

On The Other Side

We sit under a tree to catch a breeze looking in the sky wondering why no one else sees the things that we see. Night falls and the sunlight has gone so we gaze at the moon and ask why the day seemed so long. There's a look in someone's eyes as they crack a smile, laughing not crying but deep down inside their souls slowly dying. Our minds are dazed and confused as we feel disrespected and used full or worry and the vision is blurry. We accept what's in front of us and what meets the eye then were bruised with deception and defeated by lies. At times we don't listen being amazed by what glistens. We have what we need and wanting much more not being careful of what we wish for. People fake happiness and pretend to be in love but praying in silence to the heavens above. There is jealousy and envy as we read their story when you can have your desires and God's riches in glory. All though the music moves slow and life's not what it seems have faith in yourself and believe in your dreams. You may not have all you want but it's all you need so don't be fooled by what you see. If the sun's shining bright up in the sky then consider it darkness or the essential of night. Only water makes the flowers bloom and the grass is never greener on the other side.

Love

LOVE IS A STRONG FOUR letter word full of meaning. Now a day's a lot of people don't know the meaning of love. In a lot of situations the reason is because no one ever showed them real love or they were never taught how to love someone else. In order to accept love, you must know, appreciate, understand and feel love. Some people spend almost a life time accepting love from the wrong people or giving love to the wrong people. You ever wonder why some people are so bitter all the time and walk around with attitudes with the world? Sometimes it is because they feel as if they are not loved. Although they are surrounded by people who do love them, they still feel unwanted or unappreciated. When some people feel unloved, they might sometimes be angry or depressed all the time. Some people will even be hateful and hold grudges on others.

If you are loved you can feel it. Love is not just the feeling you get from being in a relationship with a man or woman. It is a feeling of comfort between family members, parents and their children, siblings, or friends. Some of the world's problems come from people that feel like no one loves them. When people have that feeling, it is hard for them to live comfortably or to love other people. You have to be very careful who you accept love from or say I love you to. Some people are very vulnerable and they take those words very seriously. The people that don't know what it is like to be loved will do almost anything to fulfill that feeling of emptiness. People that once thought they were loved and had their hearts broken will shut down in order to keep their hearts from being broken again. They do anything in their power to keep their guards up.

When a person becomes emotionally attached to someone or something, they have fallen in love with that person's character and developed a trust for them. Once that level of trust is broken, they set boundaries to make sure they can filter out the truth from lies and know who they can trust. Some people are very naïve, vulnerable, and gullible so it does not take much for them to fall in love or begin to trust people. When you say the words "I love you" say what you mean and mean what you say. Demonstrate it, show it, believe in it and most of all prove it. You only live once. Love your family, friends, those who love you and most importantly love yourself. When you find your soul mate, love beyond your wildest dreams. Don't play with someone's emotions to only destroy their inner being later on in life.

Love is based on respect, trust, honesty and it is very hard to love again once these things are destroyed beyond repair. God loves us all so we should show that same love to the people he places in our lives. Don't pretend to love someone for security purposes. Love is precious, priceless, and it is real. You can't buy love because there's no price on it. "It is a known factor that money is the root of all evil but pretending to love someone that you really don't care about is far worse.

Luke 6:35 But love your enemies, do good to them, and lend to them without expecting to get anything back. Then your reward will be great, and you will be children of the most High, because He is kind to the ungrateful and wicked. (King James Bible on Line-Luke 6:35)

Romans 12:9 love must be sincere. Hate what is evil, cling to what is good. (King James Bible on Line-Romans 12:9)

1ˢᵗ Corinthians 13: 4–8 Love is patient love is kind. It does not envy it does not boast, it is not proud. It does not dishonor others, it is not self seeking, it is not easily angered, it keeps no record of wrongs. Love does not delight in evil but rejoices with the truth. It always protects, always trusts, always hopes, it always perseveres. Love never fails. But where there are prophecies, they will cease; where there are tongues, they will be stilled. Where there is knowledge, it will pass away. (King James Bible on Line-1ˢᵗ Corinthians 13:4-8)

1ˢᵗ John 4:7 Dear friends let us love one another, for love comes from God. Everyone who loves has been born of God and knows God. (King James Bible on Line- 1ˢᵗ John 4:7)

1ˢᵗ John 4:18-19 There is no fear in love but perfect loves drives out fear, because fear had to do with punishment. The one who fears is not made perfect in love. We love because he first loved us. (King James Bible on Line-1ˢᵗ John 4:18-19)

1ˢᵗ Peter 4:8 Above all, love each other deeply because love covers a multitude of sins. (King James Bible on Line- 1ˢᵗ Peter 4:8)

(POEM)

Love is Blind

LOVE IS MORE THAN JUST flowers, candy, jewelry, and other material things. Love is long walks in the park, kissing after dark, endless conversations and fire that sparks. Love is more than just romantic evenings of wrestling in the sheets, its moments of passion, swapping secrets, and places where two souls meet. Love is not just dinner and a movie and playing games and things, it's laughing when you feel like crying and engagement rings. Love is not just fancy cars and driving long miles to say the least its knowing how to control your anger when you feel like releasing your inner beast. Love is not smiling when you're living a lie or acting just to fit in its being open and honest from beginning to end. Love is not fronting to cover up the truth it's talking things over and letting your emotions run loose. Love is hot love is cold love is beautiful love is bold love is open love is closed. Love is not screaming and yelling to get a point across or demanding and trying to be the boss its coming together and sharing your thoughts. Love is patient love is kind love is yours and love is mind love is essential and **Love Can Be Blind.**

 Trust

WE ALL KNOW THAT LIFE brings many challenges and trying times, but you have to know that there are people out there that you can trust. "There are people out there who actually care about you and what you are going through. Although it can be difficult at times to find the right people who are trust worthy, they do exist. The people you least expect to care are the ones who are most like to be there through every test and trial. We don't realize who's in our corner at times because we feel shut out. We feel closed in and afraid to let anyone into our self circle. It is because we once trusted people and they let us down that we feel we cannot confide in any one. We develop feeling of emptiness that we can't get past and it will take something or someone extraordinary for us to rebuild trust in people. We ask ourselves over and over "who can I trust? Who is in my corner? Granted we have family and friends around us daily but we still feel like no one is trustworthy. We rely on the fact that they have lives of their own so our problems will be nothing to them.

Never let life bring you to a point that you can't find anyone you can talk to, anyone to trust or like no one is willing to listen to you. There is always someone willing to listen, give advice, and help you through whatever it is that you are going through. There is always someone there who will help you build a wall of trust back up after you feel all hope is gone. Someone is out there that will help you regain trust in others. It is not easy to find comfort intrusting people when you have been let down or disappointed so many times. Trust is a virtue, and it has to be earned. You have to prove to people that you can be trusted and vice versa.

Author Experience

When I was at a breaking point in my life I didn't know who to turn to. I was unsure of who I could trust. "I was afraid to confide in people because I had been let down so many times." I didn't understand why life brought on so many challenges and nobody understood what I was going through. I knew God was with me but at times I felt as if he had given up on me. The more I went through the weaker my mind became. I sometimes couldn't even pray because I felt like I couldn't get a prayer across. "I almost started believing that life had no purpose, like it had no meaning." I thought that no matter who I talked to, no one would listen." I was certain that no one would understand me because they had never walked in my shoes.

The Struggle is Real

WHY DON'T SOME PEOPLE UNDERSTAND the basics of life? Some people would rather hang in the streets and sit around doing nothing rather than provide or contribute to the needs and wants of their families. Nothing is free in this world and some people just don't realize that. Some people find nothing wrong with living off other people and watching them struggle. Some people actually think that just their presence is good enough. There is more to life than just being there. It really puts families in a bind when you have two able bodied individuals present and one is pulling all the weight. It's hard on one person to balance between working and taking care of a family. Two able bodied individuals can pull together and make life worth living.

Why do people feel like it is okay to do absolutely nothing, to come and go as they please and then feel like someone owes them something? When you have people that depend on you, you can't sit back and watch life wither away in struggles of the world. That is not right in the eyes of God. "It is a man's duty to take care of and support his family." A man cannot live by bread alone. When you are in a household and not contributing to anything financially you are just an extra mouth to feed. Why do people feel as if they should live comfortably if they are able to gain financial stability but refuse to do anything? "Although people do it, why should people shorten their portion and the portion of the ones that depend on them, for someone who is not trying to fix the situation? Some people just have not grasped the concept of how hard it is to provide for a family and being the sole provider. "Yes it can be done, but people can have so much more if they just pull together, work together, and make an effort t have more than enough to just get by. When a household maintains more than one income, the less likely they are to struggle and have so many headaches and other problems.

It is not comfortable not knowing where your next meal is coming from or worrying about if you will have enough to pay your electric bill so you are not sitting in the dark. How can people relax in these situations? How can people feel comfortable sitting around waiting for someone else's income when they are fully capable of maintaining employment. There really has to be something wrong with a person that thinks it is ok to mooch off of other people. They must not care about life or they have lived that way for a long time and have become accustomed to it.

Some people feel like it is ok to live off government assistance. It is ok when you really hit a glitch in life and require assistance. No one should become so slack that they feel it is ok to depend on the federal government as a way of living. The amount of income they assist people with is nowhere near the amount of money it takes to live. Government assistance should be for emergency purposes and emergency purposes only. "If you are able to work you will be a lot better working to provide for yourself so you can be free and comfortable. Some people come up with all kinds of excuses not to have to work. No one is perfect and everyone will face some kind of struggle once in life. That should give people motivation to want more and do better to have their needs and wants met.

God blesses us with people that will help guide, lead, and support us. He did not intend for one person to carry the weight of the world on their shoulders. If you are married or in a relationship be the backbone and support system your partner needs to survive. Don't stand by and watch your family struggle if you are physically able to do something about it. If you are alone and struggling but do all you have to in order to survive, pat yourself on the back. In due season the struggle will be over just continue to do what it takes, believe in yourself and have faith in God.

(POEM)

Shoulder Weight

WHAT WILL I DO WHEN the waters are over my head, and I feel I have breathed my last breathes. I'll pray to God that it's just another test because I'm not ready to join the rest that failed the test and settled for less when they deserved the best and could have been blessed. I will pray, pray, pray, and pray some more until I carry out the plans He has in store and I believe what purpose is for. What will I do when I've cried my last tear trying to overcome fear like the end was near and no one cared? I will pray for strength to hold on strong cause the days seemed so long like a sad song and the beat was wrong and the tune was gone. What will I do when I'm gone with the wind because I'm tempted to sin but I know I can win because I refuse to throw the towel in after the games begin? I will pray right now I will pray today I will pray when it seems there's no way. What will I do when my burdens are heavy and the loads are not light and nothing seems right? Do I continue the fight? I will pray when the road seems rough because I'm strong and tough and I've had enough of this **SHOULDER WEIGHT STUFF.**

Loneliness

Loneliness– sadness because no one has friends or company or the quality of being unfrequented and remote; isolation (Google)

WHEN TESTS AND TRIALS WEIGH you down and bring you to a point of no return, you begin to develop a feeling of loneliness. You begin to feel as if the whole world has written you off and like you're all by yourself. It is not that you are not surrounded by people who love you, but because you feel like no one cares. You feel as if no one understands you or as if no one knows what you are going through. Being lonely sometimes comes from having your heart repeatedly broken by people you care about, or being disappointed by people you have love high hopes in. You start feeling like you are in a world all by yourself and will be that way forever. You begin to separate yourself from everybody and everything, not realizing that you are only hurting yourself. Even when you have people that care, that feeling of emptiness still torments your mind. You begin to shut down and shut people out. Some people fall into a great state of depression and even have nervous break downs.

When you begin to feel lonely, you must surround yourself with positive people who will help build you back up. You must do things that help you feel good about yourself. Be around people that you know love you and will help push you to believe in your purpose. Although it is easier said than done, you must be among people who are full of joy and laughter. Be around people who know how to enjoy life in spite of their current situations or circumstances. A lot of people who get trapped in a lonely state of mind become mentally unstable. They find it hard to cope with daily living and they shy away from the things that matter the most. They forget about things they are capable of doing. Some people even begin to believe that God has forgotten about them. They begin to feel like they have done something wrong.

Don't ever allow life to bring you to a point that you feel like the world has given up on you and you are by yourself. Don't ever feel so alone that you think you can't make it another step further in life. Sometimes God sets you apart from certain people places and things because he sees something in you that He doesn't see in other people and He wants to protect your well being. He wants to make sure you are strong before someone comes along to try to destroy your character again. He wants to protect your heart from any further hurt, harm, or other possible damage. He could be preventing you from going down a road you have already traveled. Don't be so quick to believe that you need certain people, places, and things in your life in order to feel loved or wanted. Just know that God loves you and with Him all things are possible. They very one you think is not paying you any attention, may be the one to love you more than words can say or you can ever imagine. God will love you more than life itself and make you feel like you are never by yourself. Know that you are special in the sight of God no matter who is in you corner, who walked away from you or who you had to walk away from.

Everyone experiences a feeling of loneliness at some point in life. God knows your heart and will carry you through your season of loneliness. He sets you apart from the rest sometimes to complete an assignment He has for you. God's word gives us hope and strength to handle these lonely encounters. There is someone who is closer than you think at all times. "Jesus is our comforter."

Know that there is always someone there with open arms waiting to embrace you and accept you with your emptiness.

Psalm 88:14-18 LORD, why castest thou off my soul? Why hides thou thy face from me? I am afflicted and ready to die from my youth up: while I suffer from thy terrors I am distracted. Thy fierce wrath goeth over me; thy terrors have cut me off. They came around about me daily like water; they compassed me about together. Lover and friend hast thou put far from me, and mine acquaintance into darkness. (King James Bible on Line- Psalm 88:14-18)

Psalm 38:9-15 all my longings lie before you, Lord; my sighing is not hidden from you. My heart pounds, my strength fails me; even the light had gone from my eyes. My friends and companions avoid me because of my wounds; my neighbors stay far away. Those who want to kill me set their traps, those who would harm me talk of my ruin; all day long they scheme and lie. I am the deaf, who cannot hear, the mute, who cannot speak; I have become like one who does not hear, whose mouth can offer no reply. Lord, I wait for you; you will answer Lord my God. (King James Bible on Line- Psalm 38:9-15)

(POEM)

When Will You Smile

THE FEELING OF BITTERNESS AND resentment block your inner being, you true color and who you really are. The insecurities from the pain and affliction won't carry you far. Nothings deeper than you hurt and broken pieces you carry inside and no one understands the things that you hide. When will you let go when will you smile? Torn by disappointment stands out the most afraid to love or let someone draw close. Blind to your own self worth looking over your shoulder for what's to come next emotionally disturbed but you deserve the best critically wounded so you settle for less. When will you let go when will you smile? Your soul searching, comfort seeking, faking happiness to keep your eyes from weeping. Trapped in loneliness stuck behind closed walls can refuse to move afraid to stand tall. When will you let go when will you smile? Tormented by fear and living with doubt tossing and turning like there's no way out. When will you let go when will you smile? Stop living in regret and see the best just hasn't arrived yet. Love yourself and believe for a while. When will you let go? **When will you smile?**

Teenage Pregnancy

TEEN AGE PREGNANCY HAPPENS A lot in today's society. A lot of teenage Girls get into a relationship thinking they are in love but don't really know what it is. They give no thought to what they are doing until it is too late. They find that guy who "they think is the one" and they begin to believe by some of his actions that he loves her. They fall head over heels and the next thing you know she is pregnant. In some cases he disappears and wants nothing else o do with her once he finds out. She then becomes very afraid and doesn't know which way to turn.

A lot of people assume when they see a young girl pregnant that she was not raised right. "That is not always the case." A lot of times these young girls do come from families at love and care for them. They are just taking life at its' daily challenges and explore what the world has to offer before they really should. Some of them simply rebel against what they are told or taught because someone whispered sweet nothings in their ears. Someone somewhere convinced, pressured or persuaded them into thinking that it was ok to have sex even though they were not married and financially stable. Someone probably made them feel as if they would be missing something if they didn't. They feel as if they don't give into their boyfriend then another girl will and they will lose him to that other girl.

Some young girls do know what they are doing but they just don't care because they are or they think they are grown and have it all together. They don't wake up until it is too late and they are pregnant and don't know which way to turn. They know their parents or guardians will be upset and disappointed and they might have consequences for their actions. Some of them become afraid of what others might think of them. They are confused and don't know who to turn to for help. "They don't know who to trust at this point." Some of them might even try running away from home not realizing that it will only make matters worse in the end. "Young girls if you find yourself in this situation don't run from the people who will be with you no matter the outcome." Remember that you are loved and God sees, hears and knows everything about you. He will not leave nor forsake you no matter how the outside world looks at you. Know that the people you think will turn their back on you will be the ones there to help you along life's bumpy roads. The people you try to confide in might be the ones to turn their backs on you.

Although parents or guardians want what's best for their children, they have to realize these things happen all over the world today. No matter how much you preach, teach, and tell them to concentrate on education first, it does not always turn out that way. Don't ever think you are exempt from the situation because it happens to the best of people. Although we know these young people need to set goals, and conquer their dreams first, the world always throws stumbling blocks in their way. People on the outside looking in should not in any way discourage these young people into believing that life is over for them due to their circumstances. Don't make them think or feel as if they have failed at life or life has failed them. There has to be someone out there somewhere to reel them back in and let them know that life in not over for them and they still have a chance to get it right. They need to know that they can still be successful, persevere, and reach their highest potential. Let them know that they can do all things through Christ who strengthens them. They need moral support or they will seek attention elsewhere. They will look to people who will feed them false hope and shattered dreams. Yes they will face many challenges and have to work harder to accomplish their goals but they can do it. It is possible if someone keeps them lifted up and let them know that life has meaning before, during, and after the storm.

Young ladies if you have children at a young age know that you still have opportunities to set and achieve goals. No one is perfect in this world and people fall short of God's gory on a daily basis. Although people might tell you babies are a mistake, know that they are a blessing from above. The mistake is in the sin that was committed not in an innocent baby but God is a forgiving God. If you are faced with a tough decision when in this situation, make sure you seek the proper help and do what's best for you in the long run. This is your life and people can help you but no one can live your life for you. Make sure you embrace the love, encouragement an\d assistance from those that are there to support you no matter what you decide. Respect your support system. Be obedient to your parents, guardians, or people who have been where you are. Trust and appreciate those who will provide for you and your child. In most cases they will not stir you in the wrong direction. Do not worry about outsiders. Some people will try to discourage you but they don't matter because they are not in your shoes and will offer you nothing not even advice. Be mindful of the things you will face and what's to come thereafter. In all things trust God and know that He is the Alpha and Omega the beginning and the end. Know that He is the creator of all things and good things come to those who love and trust Him.

Author Experience

At the age of sixteen, I got pregnant. I was not at all comfortable with the situation and I was not pleased with myself at all. I had not finished school and I felt like I would be a failure. Needless to say I did not have a baby at the age of sixteen, I had a miscarriage. I was very hurt and confused and didn't really understand what happened or why it happened. I was depressed and stressed out for a long time after that. I had to eventually bounce back and come to the realization that it wasn't in God's timing it wasn't in His will for my life that I have a baby that early in my life. He had other plans for my life. Sometimes we don't understand His plans but we must trust him and not question his works because he knows what's best for us in the end and He makes no mistakes. "I became a grandmother at a young age and wouldn't trade it in for the world."

Relationships/Cheating

HAVE YOU EVER BEEN IN relationship that you felt like the other person didn't really care about or love you? Even though you felt like that you tried to make yourself believe they did care. If you have ever felt like that, in some cases it was because you were right, that feeling was real. If you are ever in a relationship and start feeling like that, it is time to do some research. Sometimes people will love you for all the wrong reasons to include security purposes, a lot of times it is because they know what you are capable and what you can or will do for them. Some people spend a lot of time trying to find all the good in a relationship because they don't want to believe the other person does not really love or care for them. Relationships will turn out a lot better if people do some research in the beginning. Falling in love doesn't happen overnight.

Most people have dreams of falling in love with the right person or finding their soul mate and spending the rest of their life with them. Life does not always turn out that way. Some people experience a least one bad relationship before they find the right person to be in a good relationship with. In order to make a relationship work out for the better, you have to set boundaries at the beginning. In order to beat the odds of having your feelings crushed in a relationship, you must follow some basic steps.

1. Know what you want out of life
2. Know what you expect out of a relationship or your partner
3. Know the things that are tolerable
4. Gain knowledge of your partner and what they want out of life
5. Be up front in the beginning and put your expectations on the table
6. Find things you both like to do in leisure time
7. Always make time for each other outside of busy lifestyles
8. Be understanding and passionate about feelings
9. Understand their past
10. Hold each other up through hard times, struggles, and difficulties
11. Love one another unconditionally.

Every relationship has its ups and downs but if both hearts are in it for the long haul, the more the chances of the relationship being successful. If two hearts are not on the same level, it won't always work out. "Two god hearts make a great team." Without love and trust there is no relationship no matter how hard you try. We must not be blind to the fact that real love is transparent. If a person doesn't really love you it will show. You can see it, ear it, and most importantly you should be able to feel it. Always make time to explore a person's past before you invest your time into a future with them. Everything that glitters is not gold and everything that sparkles does not always shine. A person will paint a pretty picture in the beginning of a relationship. "They are always fronting for the camera. Never second guess your intuition. Lay all your cards on the table from the start. Understand a person before you accept them.

You ever wonder how a person can cheat on someone they have been in a relationship with for years? Husbands cheat on wives and vice versa. How can people cheat on someone they claim to love and plan on spending the rest of their life with? This is a question asked all over the world today. It is one of the many questions no one has an answer to. Cheating is one of the Leading causes of breakups, separations, or divorces in marriages. No one actually has a legitimate explanation as to why they cheat. Instead they have all kinds of excuses, after they get caught. "An excuse is not an answer." Cheating comes from one trying to fulfill or satisfy their sinful lusts or their own flesh.

In this cold world we live in a cheater will try hard to not own up to his or her wrong doings. They come up with a thousand and one ways to justify their actions. Sometimes they even try to live their way out after being caught. Some people don't realize what they are doing in the heat of the moment or they just don't care. They dint realize what they are jeopardizing. Who wants to be in a relationship with someone who is always cheating? When you cheat you are selling yourself short of what life has to offer in a committed relationship. Cheating causes insecurities and is also known as infidelity. It is being unfaithful and disloyal. Cheating makes people feel like they are not good enough and causes them to develop low self esteem. When they get in another relationship it's hard for them to trust the other person.

People wait for answers to cheating because it happens so often. A cheater will look the person they claim to love right in the face, tell them they love them knowing they have cheated. Does that mean they do not love their spouse or partner? I guess only a cheater will have an answer for that question. Cheating takes people on an emotional roller coaster ride. There is no stability in a relationship if there is not trust. Trust and respect are the ties that bind a relationship. Let's be honest, who wants to stay in a relationship or marriage if you lay awake every night and wonder where your other half is? Most of the emotional roller coasters in relationship come from cheating and being unfaithful.

Marriage and relationships are more than just sex. If you find someone who will always have your back and be there for you no matter what, cherish them. If a person is not constantly lying to you and doing things to hurt you embrace their loyalty. You need someone to trust and can depend on at all times. If you are in a relationship and get cheated on don't lose your self esteem or self worth searching for answers. Just know that there is someone out there for everybody and in due time god will send you someone who will sweep you off your feet.

People of God don't miss out on the finer things in a relationship by cheating and not being faithful. Once you are in a relationship and say you love someone, you should be devoted, committed and ready to endure endless happiness with that person. Cheating will cause you to lose focus and miss out on the blessings God has in store for you.

Author Experience

I know what it is like to be cheated on and to have your heart repeatedly broken. I was cheated on several times. I was to a point that I couldn't understand for the life of me why this kept happening to me. I was very hurt, confused and couldn't function at times. It caused me to develop low self esteem and it made me feel like I was worthless. A one point I started believing there was something wrong with me. I had to ask myself why I kept getting hurt in the midst of trying to give my all to someone. It was destroying my inner being. I was at a point that I felt I wasn't good enough for anyone. I felt betrayed disrespected, disappointed and set apart from the rest of the world. I started telling myself that no one loved me or would ever love me. My mind was tormented by insecurities. I had to pray and seek God for answers. **Thank God for his love, kindness, faithfulness, grace, and mercy.**

1st Corinthians 6:9 Know ye that the unrighteous shall not inherit the kingdom of God? Be not deceived: neither fornicators, nor idolaters, nor adulterers, nor effeminate, nor abusers of themselves with mankind, nor thieves, nor covetous, nor drunkards, nor revilers, nor extortions, shall inherit the kingdom of God. (King James Bible on Line-1ˢᵗ Corinthians 6:9)

James 4:4 Ye adulterers and adulteresses, know ye not the friendship of the world is enmity with God? Whosoever therefore will be a friend of the world is the enemy of God. (King James Bible on Line-James 4:4)

Hebrews 13:4 marriage is honorable in all, and the bed undefiled: but whoremongers and adulterers, God will judge. (Kings James Bible on Line-Hebrews 13:4)

Luke 18:11 The Pharisee stood and prayed thus with himself, God, I thank thee, that I am not as other men are extortioners, unjust, adulterers, or even the publican. (King James Bible on Line-Luke 18:11)

Malachi 3:5 And I will come near to you to judgement; and I will be a swift witness against the sorcerers, and against the adulterers, and against false swearers, and against those that oppress the hireling in his wages, the widow, and the fatherless, and that turn aside the stranger from his right, and fear not me, saith the Lord of hosts. (King James bible on Line Malachi 3:5)

(POEM)

I Tossed My Wedding Ring

THERE CAME A POINT IN life that I had to give up the fight life was no longer comfortable and nothing seemed right. I could have lost everything because I didn't have anything so I had to fly with my own two wings. I didn't realize the joy that it would bring once I started doing my own thing and following my dreams. I had to separate myself from people places and things and act like a human being so I tossed my wedding ring. Although I had to swim the ocean and cross the deep blue sea, fly with the wind and flow with the breeze that came from the trees I was determined to find the real me. I never knew that life could be so sweet after being so weak and stumbling over my own two feet. I had to escape the broken promises and the acts of being dishonest because it was breaking me down when no one was around and robbing me of the joy I thought I had found. It got so scary that I began to get weary and I didn't believe in the fairy God mother or the tooth fairy. I had to separate myself from people places and things and act like a human being so I tossed my wedding ring. It all seemed so wrong but I had to be strong I had to move on and sing my own song if I wanted to live long. I refused to look back I had to keep moving if not I would simply start losing and suffer from mental abuse that would cause permanent bruising. I had to listen and take heed to what I learned to stay strong and keep from getting burned. I had to show people that now it was my turn. I looked to God from the heavens above cause I knew He would show me real love and grant me blessings I never thought of. I never knew life would treat me like that until I turned my back and walked away from the bull crap. I had to separate myself from people places and things and act like a human being so **I tossed my wedding Ring**.

Confidence- The feeling or belief that one can rely on someone or something; firm trust

The state of feeling certain about the truth of something

A feeling of self-assurance arising from one's appreciation of one's own abilities or qualities

In order to be successful in life and it is very important that we have confidence in ourselves, the things we believe in, our dreams, our goals, and the things we are capable of. We have to take pride in the things we set out to accomplish. Being confident gives us motivation to do better, be better, do our best and strive for perfection. A lack of confidence in one's self will surely kill our dreams. "Don't your own dream killer." It is a known fact that we have people on the outside looking in that will try to destroy our dreams or the things we believe in. If we let go of our shield of confidence we will start believing the negative things that other people say about us.

Sometimes we don't realize we have a purpose in life because we have such little confidence. This sometimes comes from the things we have been through. Certain situations and circumstances have a tendency of making us doubt ourselves as well as God's plan. Once we start doubting we lose all hope as well as our self confidence. We must realize that we go through things sometimes to develop a clearer understanding of who we are and who God says we are. It is very difficult for one to gain mental stability if he or she has no self confidence. Always be confident in yourself so you can better any situation. Our confidence will help other people build their own confidence.

People of God build great confidence in yourself and believe that you have a purpose in life. Don't let your current or past situations distract you from your dreams. God makes no mistakes. Some people will let their faith slip away because they are not confident enough to withstand the tests of times. Although it may take some people longer than others, building confidence is imperative to every human being. Without confidence some people become failures, statistics, and what others say we will be. Having confidence gives us strength to carry on in spite of what things might look like or what others think.

Philippians 1:6 for I am confident of this very thing, that He who began a good work in you will perfect it until the day of Jesus Christ. (King James Bible on Line-Philippians 1:6)

Hebrews 4:16 Therefore let us draw near with confidence to the throne of grace, so that we may receive mercy and find grace to help in time of need. (King James Bible on Line-Hebrews 4:16)

Proverbs 3:26 for the lord will be your confidence and will keep your foot from being caught. (King James Bible on Line-Proverbs 3:26)

1st John 5:14 This is the confidence which we have before him, that, is we ask anything according to His will, He hears us.(King James Bible on Line- 1st John 5:14)

Single Parenting

SOMETIMES LIFE THROWS SO MUCH in your lap at one time that you hardly have time to relax, breathe, or focus on yourself. Being a single parent is not what everyone wishes and hopes for, but it is sometimes how things are. Single parenting is one of the hardest jobs a person can have. Although a lot of people are great at it, it can be very weight bearing and overwhelming at times. Single parents carry the weight of the world on their shoulders but cannot give up because they have people that depend on them. They have people who rely on their strength to make it through every day. There are daily challenges to being a single parent and they can be very stressful at times. A single parent wears many titles they are doctors, lawyers, school teachers, counselors, referees, cooks, house maids, hair dressers, and much more. Sometimes they have many qualifications. They have patience, kindness, meekness, dependability, faithfulness, and patience. Many people over look the power of a single parent. It might not seem like much to some, but single parents have a lot on their plate. They have to juggle between working to take care of home and providing accurate leader ship, love and guidance to their children.

Not all single parents are in that situation by choice. Some are in that situation because they could have lost their better half, or their relationship and or marriage simply did not work out. Some people choose to be single parents because they did not have the moral, physical, financial, or emotional support they needed from their partner to have a family. In that case they decided it was best to do it alone. Often times when you are by yourself, you wonder if you are doing a good enough job. You question if you are setting a good enough example for your children to do the right thing. As a single parent you must always dedicate your time and attention when it is necessary. Single parents must watch what they do In front of their children. Know that your children are watching you even when you think they are not paying attention. There are times that you might have to sacrifice to make ends meet. If you have not walked in the shoes of a single parent then you do not know their daily struggles. Single parents have to remain strong even through their breaking points.

God sometimes have single parents in that situation because He knows where your strength lies. He knows that you have what it takes to withstand the toughest of storms. Children of single parents must realize that individual was places in your life for a reason. Do single parents always have the right answers? No but they will research and find answers to everything. They have to be reliable and make their selves available at all times. There are various roads that single parents have to travel. Some travel them with a grain of salt while others opt to give up and throw in the towel. Everyone needs time to sit and regroup but single parents "never lose focus on the things that are required of you." Single parents need to be told and reminded that they are doing a great job if that's what they are doing. Single parents know that no matter how hard things may seem God will supply your every need. When he supplies you with the necessary tools you need, use them to the best of your ability. Don't ever allow life to defeat your purpose. Even though certain situations may make you feel as if you have failed as a parent, don't give up. "You can only fail in life if you refuse to keep trying."

Author Experience

Being a single parent was a very trying and difficult time in my life. "I would be telling a lie if I said it was easy." I ran into more hard times than I ever anticipated. "Although I often felt like I failed at being a mother, failure was not an option for me." Everyday brought new challenges and more experiences. Even though I struggled, I always remained a go getter. There were times that I would sit in silence and drift away in my thoughts but I had to bounce back and realize that some people didn't make it that far. I became a single parent when I realized that "even when I wasn't single I was still a single mother."

Know your Worth

PEOPLE OFTEN WONDER WHY OLDER men find comfort in sleeping with "young girls." Everyone is entitled to their own opinion, but I really don't think that is attractive at all. There is no way in this world should a fifty year old man be sleeping with a fifteen year old. "She is a child, she is someone's daughter, someone's baby." Even though some young girls act like they are grown, does not give an old man the right to treat her like she is. There are various reasons theses young girls act out like that. They might be looking for a father figure because daddy is not there anymore and they desire that fatherly attention. Some young girls might do it for money because they are in families that struggle. Someone somewhere might have told these young girls that it was ok to sleep with older men because they will take care of them.

These old men should be classifies as perverts because they are fulfilling their own sexual lusts by sleeping with a young girl who hasn't even had a shot at living life yet. Why do they have to pay young girls to sleep with them when there are women out there their ages they can sleep with? Some of these men actually have wives and families at home and still do it. "They actually pay young girls for sex." I don't think I'm by myself when I say that is perversion.

No matter how people look at this situation it is also a form of manipulation. An older person has the tendency to be able to manipulate the mind of a young child." That is a form of molestation, sexual abuse, or statutory rape no matter how people look at it. It can also be considered prostitution if there is money involved. There are even people out there giving young children away to older men for money. That is human trafficking. Some people don't take these issues seriously but it is becoming a bigger problem daily all over the world even in places we don't think it's going on. A lot of these situations are not talked about because people are afraid, ashamed or simply know it's wrong but don't care. Not everyone looks on these situations the same and some see no problem with it. Some will just say well "she likes older men, or he likes younger women but when she's under the age of 18 she is still a child. I believe a lot of these young girls are easily persuaded and are being bribed with money.

If these young girls are being taken advantage of and not saying anything it is because they are being told not to say anything. These old men have lived their lives and probably have been in numerous relationships. The reason they keep it hid is because they know there are consequences if the wrong individuals find out what is going on. Some parents will actually resort to physical harm or maybe even murder when or if they find out their teenage daughter is being taken advantage of by an older man. Others will just get law enforcement involved. Young girls should have the opportunity to experience what life has to offer on their own and not be taken advantage of by someone who has lived life. "Some old men just corrupt the minds of young girls and I find it very sickening, wrong and disrespectful. "You ever wonder how they would feel if it were their own child?" It makes me wonder if they have daughters and may have done it to them.

Some men really need to pay more attention to their daughters, and love them unconditionally because if not they will look for that love elsewhere. These young girls are looking for a father figure so they find comfort in being with older men. In some cases young girls are just rebellious, promiscuous and just want to explore the world and all its tactics. Grown men need to consider the fact that these young ladies have families that love and care for them and want the best for them. Some parents have no knowledge of what's going on with their children because it remains a secret. Let's be honest how often does a teenage girl bring a fifty year old man home and say this is my boyfriend?

Young ladies of you find yourself falling for the schemes and games of an older man know that these men have already experienced life and only desire one thing from you. They will do almost anything to get it. Half of them are probably marries in a relationship or have children of their own. If you are looking for love, a friendship, or a companion, find someone your age or around your age so you can build together and experience life together. Learn to be patient, wait on God and put your trust in Him first. Know how to separate the father of all lies from the truth that will make you free and keep you from all hurt and danger. No matter what you're going through or how things look, don't be easily persuaded into doing something that you will later on in life regret. Don't be talked into doing something that makes you feel uncomfortable or uneasy. Don't lose self worth pride or dignity for anything or anyone. Don't ever let "anyone" make you do things you feel are not right or don't want to do. Don't except gifts or money in exchange for your most valuable possessions. You unique, fearfully and wonderfully made and God will give you the desires of your heart in due season.

Child Molestation

IT IS REALLY SICK WHEN someone takes advantage of small innocent children. There are child molesters everywhere. You ever wonder when the world went wrong or how these sick minded beasts came from. Child molesters just suck the life out of people who have no control of the situation. This is something that gets kept in the dark in some cases for a long period of time. We often wonder why children hide the fact that they have been taken advantage of. It is simply because they are made uncomfortable and feel like they may have done something wrong. Some people are so manipulative that they torment the minds of these young innocent children. Most of these monsters have control of the situation so they persuade these children into not saying anything. Child molesters make children feel there is nothing wrong with touching, feeling, or doing things that are inappropriate. "These individuals should be places under a jail cell.

Child molestation is something that can affect people for the rest of their lives. Even though they hardly ever talk about it, it can really destroy their inner being as well as their conscious. It's something that some individuals carry over into their adulthood. Although people think they have gotten over it, it is something that takes a life time to heal. It causes people to not be able to trust others that are around them. Some people have to go through a lifetime of therapy and other counseling. Victims of child molestation look at other people and wonder if they have been in that situation being the victim or the perpetrator.

Author Experience

After living all my life with the torment of being molested by several people, this awful experience followed me to my adulthood. "I told part of my story in my first book." Living with this torment in my mind, I always looked at people and wondered who they really were. I just was never comfortable around too many people no matter who they were. I had a very disturbed conscious and I didn't trust anyone. It was so bad that people would be talking to me and it looked like I was listening but my mind was all over the place. Even with my relationships, I always felt like I was doing something wrong. "I can honestly say to people that have been through the pain of being molested, that I feel their pain." I know how you feel I understand the torment in the back of your mind. Know that in due season God will heal those open wounds. It might take time but all things are possible through Christ who strengthens us. He will never leave nor forsake you. Some people don't make it far after this awful experience. They turn to drugs and alcohol and some even commit suicide. Some people are just not strong enough to endure the pain of having their innocence snatched from them. Some people have also turned into the victimizer. "Children of God open up your hearts and allow him to heal those open wounds."

Emotional Trauma

EMOTIONAL TRAUMA IS ALSO KNOWN as psychological trauma. (Google) It is a type of damage to the mind that occurs as a result of a severely frightening or distressing event.(Google) Trauma is often the result of an over whelming amount of stress that exceeds one's ability to cope with or integrate the emotions involved with that experience.(Google) It is also the injury to the psyche after living through a painful event.(Google) It may result in challenges in functioning or coping normally after the event. (Google) It is the unique individual experience or an event or enduring conditions, in which: the individual's ability to integrate his/her emotional experience is overwhelmed, or the individual experiences a threat to life, bodily integrity, or sanity.(Google)

Roughly seventy percent of the world will suffer from some type of emotional trauma. There are emotional and physical signs and symptoms of emotional trauma. Some are poor concentration, paleness, fatigue, lethargy, and a racing heartbeat. Some physical symptoms are physical injury or illness. In order to manage stress after a traumatic event, people should be very well taken care of. Some people have anxiety or panic attacks and are unable to come with certain circumstances. Some common symptoms of trauma are denial, anger, sadness, and outbursts. People who have endured trauma experiences can be disoriented. They may not respond to conversation like they normally do.

Victims of emotional trauma redirect the emotions towards other people like friends or family. That makes trauma very difficult for loved ones as well as the victim. It can be very hard to help people if they push you away and refuse your help. Understanding tier emotions help in the process. The effects are either long or short it can be weeks or even years before they bounce back. Some people who suffer trauma may have to take medication. If depression becomes an issue it may be treated with antidepressants. Many trauma victims also suffer from anxiety and take anti-anxiety medication. Medication options depend on the individual's medical history.

People if you or a loves one suffers or is suffering from any kind of emotional trauma, know that there is help available. There is a variety of treatment and other resources out there to help through the process. There are caring people and professionals out there who are willing to help. Sometimes the recovery outlook can turn out good. Often times the most important thing is getting help with the first step. Untreated trauma can resort t some lifelong experiences. Depression can become too much to cope with. Victims of trauma are more likely to develop addictions than other general populations of people. Family and friends of victims should look out for signs of addiction after trauma has occurred. No matter the situation they need to be open minded to what their loved one has suffered and realize that they are looking for ways t overcome emotions. Some people are able to bounce back from trauma while others have a hard time. They search for ways to ease the pain. Those on the outside looking in must become helpers and do not judge. The bible gives us comfort in knowing that if we trust in God He will be our healer, deliverer and shelter from any storm.

Psalm 107:13-16 Then they cried to the Lord in their trouble, and He delivered them from their distress. He brought them out of darkness and the shadow of death, and burst their bonds apart.

Let them thank the Lord for his steadfast love, for his wondrous works to the children of man! (King James Bible on Line-Psalm 107:13-16)

Isaiah 41:10 Far not, for I am with you; be not dismayed, for I am your God; I will strengthen you, I will help you, I will uphold you with my righteous right hand. (King James Bible on Line-Isaiah 41:10)

Matthew 11:28-30 Come to me, all who labor and are heavy laden, and I will give you rest. Take my yoke upon you, and learn from me, for I am gentle and lowly in heart. And you will find rest for your souls. "For my yoke is easy, ad my burden is light. (King James Bible on Line-Matthew 11:28-30)

Joel 2:25 I will restore to you the years that the swarming locust has eaten, the hopper the destroyer, and the cutter, my great army, which I sent among you. (King James Bible on Line-Joel 2:25)

Temptation

DON'T EVER BE SO BLINDED by what's in
front of you that you can't tell the difference between good,
bad, evil, right or wrong. Some people go a long time in life
letting other's dictate to them how life should be by painting a
pretty picture for them. They take the wrong turn and make bad
decisions before they realize what is best for them in the end. A lot
of times we blame the enemy when our life is not making sense.
In some cases the enemy will try us and put things before us that
look like they are not detrimental to us. The enemy will try us
when he knows that we are trying to live right and he realizes
that we have purpose in life. When we are prone to doing the will
of God is when he will try us the most. He knows just how to
set people up for failure. If people are not careful of the lifestyles
they live, they will find themselves falling subject to the snares
and the traps set by the enemy. "He has many traps set for God's
people." Does the enemy have to try us when we are already
engaging in sin? Let's just say if we are living in sin then we are
already walking in his footsteps.

No one wants to admit it when they are not living right
because a lot of people believe in their hearts that some things
are not a sin or an abomination. "Who are we to Judge?" for
example we have people's that live a gay lifestyle. Some of these
people might be living that way because they have been hurt by

someone of the opposite sex and they have found love and comfort in someone of the same sex. "We have to let God be the judge." We never know why people live a certain way. Although it is not right in the sight of God, everyone has their own beliefs. People must not be tempted by the things they know are wrong but look right in their eyes! Temptation comes when we don't pay attention to our surroundings. How many times have we been tempted to try new things in life? How many times did we fall for it?

Some women find comfort in sleeping with numerous men and some men find comfort in sleeping with many women. This happens sometimes when people are searching for the right one because life has failed them so many times. Although past relationships bring us pain and affliction, we must not be tempted to search for love in all the wrong places. Some people are actually infatuated by sex that they are not satisfied in just one person. This is a trick of the enemy. Ladies men do not respect you if you have been with too many men. You have to be an extraordinary person with great character and integrity otherwise you will be labeled as everything other than a child of God. Men if you sleep with many women and have developed that reputation a real woman will not want you.

The bible clearly tells us that he who finds a wife finds a good thing. "People of God stop looking for love and comfort in sex. Make people respect your character. Ladies let a man be able to look at you and say "now that is a good woman."

People are so fooled by lies and deception these days that they lose focus on which way to turn. Temptation is a trick of the enemy. Satan is the father of all lies. We must not be tempted or mislead by things that glow in the natural eye. "Everything that glitters is not gold and everything that sparkles does not always shine. "We must be able to distinguish right from wrong. We must be able to separate those things that are meant to break us down and destroy us from the things that will sustain us. We must be able to determine the truth and understand the difference from righteousness and living in sin. Be able to realize a trap from the enemy by being spiritually inclined to do God's will.

In some cases people are so bound up in sin, lies and what is in front of them that they will accept whatever is thrown at them. They will get wrapped up in a relationship or friendship with people knowing that their lifestyle is headed for destruction. "Although we don't like to face reality, we have to get our lives right, and lined up with the word of God. We must put on the whole armor of God. If we are not careful of our environment or surroundings at all times, "we will surely fall subject to the enemies traps. We must get in tune with his tactics so he has nothing to use against us. An example of this is someone falling in love with a drug addict or alcoholic. If we are not careful and suited up for battle, we might be pulled into the same things. "Some people are just quick at believing if they engage in the same thing as someone else that it will make them love them more. "Don't join the party if it is not your type of party." Temptation comes in all different ways, shapes, forms, and fashions.

People of God know that if someone loves you they will not offer or present you with something that is going to destroy or ruin your life. By any means if they do, you must use the strength God gives you to say no and resist temptation. Try to help them help themselves. Love is not meant to destroy your character or ruin your life. It is meant to build you up and add greatness to who God says you are. Understand that sleeping with people just to prove a point is a trap of the enemy and it will not make anyone fall in love with you. "It is being tempted as you feel passion in the heat of the moment and its lusting or satisfying the flesh. God is love and His love will not cause you any harm.

Don't be so tempted by what is in front of you that you lose focus on your future and success. Temptation is the hardest part of every battle. If you have lost the battle with temptation, then realize that the real battle has yet to come. When you resist temptation it shows that you have strength to persevere no matter what is in front of you, and you can overcome every obstacle that stands in your way. Know that when you have resisted temptation you have what it takes to conquer all your fears. The enemy wants you to believe there is nothing wrong with the sin you are committing so he can have his way in your life. He knows God has a plan for you and he wants to be sure to torment you to a point of no return.

Psalm 95:8 harden not your heart, as in the provocation, and as in the day of temptation in the wilderness. (King James Bible on Line-Psalm 95:8)

Matthew 6:13 and leas us not into temptation, but deliver us from evil: For thine is the kingdom, and the power, and the glory, forever. Amen (King James Bible on Line-Matthew 6:13)

Matthew 26:41 Watch and pray that ye enter not into temptation. The spirit is truly ready, but the flesh is weak. (King James bible on Line-Matthew 26:41)

Mark 14:38 Watch ye and pray, lest ye enter into temptation. The spirit is truly ready, but the flesh is weak. (King James Bible on Line- Mark 14:38)

Luke 4:13 And when the devil has ended all the temptation, he departed from him for a season. (King James Bible on Line-Luke 4:13)

Luke 8:13 They on the rock are they, which, when they hear, receive the word with joy; and these have no root, which for a while believe, and in time of temptation fall away. (King James Bible on Line-Luke 8:13)

Luke 11:4 And forgive us or sins; for we also forgive everyone that is indebted to us. And lead us not into temptation; but deliver us from evil. (King James Bible on Line-Luke 11:4)

Luke 22:40 And when he was at the place, he said unto them, Pray that ye enter not into temptation. (King James Bible on Line-Luke 22:40)

Luke 22:46 And said unto them, Why sleep ye? rise and pray, lest ye enter into temptation. (King James Bible on Line-Luke 22:46)

1ˢᵗ Corinthians 10:13 There hath no temptation taken you but such is as common to man: but God is faithful, who will not suffer you to be tempted above that ye are able; but will with the temptation also make a way to escape, that e may be able to bear it. (King James Bible on Line-1ˢᵗ Corinthians 10:13)

(POEM)

That's Not the Way

ALCOHOL WON'T SAVE THE DAY, a crack pipe won't ease the pain, heroine will only replace the cocaine that won't erase what happened yesterday. Sex or a baby won't make him stay so choose a better way and walk away before the voices in your head drive you insane. You only get one life to live so live how you want to live, but don't blame the world for the things you chose or the things you did. You had freedom to choose but you choose to lose STOP trying to walk in the next man's shoes. He can't save you from a world of sin and he's still looking for a way to fit in wondering when his pain will end. You better head in another direction. You were on the right path so exactly what happened? Get yourself together and come off that get high binge. You might lose everything your family your friends. Get some rehab or maybe counseling Staying up all not just ant right you're on the verge or suicide then your family cry as they say good bye. Alcohol won't save the, day crack won't take the pain away sex and a baby won't make him stay so choose a better way before you go insane and that's not the way.

Through the Storm

SOMETIMES LIFE TAKES YOU ON a roller coaster ride that is unexpected, with lots of bumps and bruises. It will have you thinking and believing that life has no meaning after the rain. When the storms of life are raging and you see no way out, your mind is like a thunderstorm. We wait and listen for the next set of noises. We stare at the drops as they become larger and larger. We try to wear protective gear to keep from getting completely drenched and soaked. We must protect our feet from the muddy puddles we might have to walk through. We must realize that even through the toughest storm, our prize can sometimes be hidden in the mud. "If you ever been through anything in life you will understand that." If not then don't try to figure it out.

After we go through storms in life, we sit, reflect back, then we wonder how we made it through alive. We wonder how we made it through hurt, pain, frustration and more. We wonder how we made it through struggles tests, heart breaks and disappointments. We try to figure out how we made it through health issues, temptation, trials and tribulations. How did we make through alive? There are just so many changes and transitions people go through when they are trying to weather a storm. A lot of people have to make sacrifices in order to come better than before. When you go through a storm in life you sit back and think of the people who have written you off or the people you had to let go of. We remember what we did to let them go and how hard it was. Oftentimes we sit and wonder what certain people think of us now. We go through much before, during, and a storm that we wonder if we made the right choices or followed the right steps. We wonder if we hurt along the journey and we sometimes suffer with fear and doubt.

After the storm we shout try not to look back at what once was, what should have or could have been. Sometimes we are reminded of those things because certain situations will bring them back to our memory. We must know that we came through the storm with God on our side and He remains in our corner faithful and trustworthy. People of God know that if various storms didn't break you then you overcame the things that were meant to destroy you. When God walks with you through the storm, sometimes it is hard for you to even recognize that He is there. When everything is crumbling right before your eyes, it gives you no choice but to believe that there is no shelter from the storm. We seek many ways to overcome and we seek hiding places so we don't have to face our fears and challenges. We search for the right people we can talk to and who we can trust. "Even in our darkest hour we must recognize that God is listening and he hears our cries.

When life serves you nothing but lemons know that there are endless possibilities. There are millions of ways to overcome and weather the storm. Whoever said that life will always be great certainly didn't know what they were saying because you will always be tried in the fire. It is when you start to see the finer things in life that you gain motivation. Just know that God knows you are a conqueror and He wouldn't allow you to go through the things you go through if he didn't believe in you. Only the strong survive and those that seek wisdom, knowledge and understanding will prosper.

Author Experience

When the storms in my life were raging, I felt as if life was over for me. I didn't trust anyone. I didn't know who to turn to or who I could confide in. I didn't know who would listen and give me advice or who would laugh at me then turn their backs on me. Even though my character showed no emotion because I covered it up with smiles and laughter, "life had no meaning to me." I cried until I couldn't cry another tear. I knew I needed to pray but that was hard. I understood that prayer was the answer but I couldn't see past the hurt, pain and suffering. Although people told me to seek the Lord it was easier said than done. I always looked at people and wondered if they really knew what was on the inside of me. There was nothing anyone said or did that made me believe that life wad meaning. It was only when I called upon the Lord with my whole heart that I began to see life for what it was and realize that He cares.

Don't be Pulled from your Purpose

THERE COMES A TIME IN life that you have to see yourself in God's image. View yourself as He sees you. Don't let your past disappointments and failures distract you from your destiny or what God has for you. Don't allow the manipulations and interruptions that are planted in your mind and heart determine your future. Everyone goes through things that might make them feel less than they are worth but we determine our self worth. Know that god has a perfect will and does things in perfect timing. He has a purpose for you, you, and you. Don't lose focus on your purpose for people places and things that have no value or morals in life. People will do anything to pull you from your purpose.

If you didn't have a purpose in life, God would have let you drown in the midst of your worries. The same people who try to pull you from your purpose, or take you out of character are the same people who have no integrity and will one day be your biggest fan. They are going to wonder how you made it to the top in spite of what you been through. The will want to be a part of what God is doing in your life. Sometimes when we sit and look back over our life we wonder how we made it to our purpose. Then we realize it was the Love of God and his hands that He never took off of us. He was us in the midst of our long sufferings. Some people spend almost an entire lifetime not knowing they have purpose in life or simply not caring that they do have purpose. They have allowed the world to pull the purpose out of them.

Don't be that individual that has let life suck the purpose out f you. "I can't say it enough." Don't let the enemy take what was meant for your good and destroy it to a point of no return. Sometimes it takes some people longer than others to discover their purpose. But when they do, "Oh what a joyous occasion." We all have a purpose in life if we didn't we not have made it this far. Be the individual that lives to talk about your purpose, how you discovered it, and help other people discover their purpose. Know that God will lead you to your purpose in due season. What is your purpose? Have you discovered it yet?

(POEM)

Your Life

PEOPLE TRY TO STEAL YOUR gratitude to adjust your attitude but don't know what it feels like to be you. They watch you as you move and mimic what you do but couldn't walk a mile in your shoes. They try to turn contentment into endless resentment but never read how your story ended. They are always mad at you never glad for you never sad for you but don't know why you do the things that you do. They gather in circles and constantly talk but refuse to understand why you walk like you walk. You're always to blame when they slander your name and try to run game and that is a shame. They can't think like you think or blink like you blink so they try to make you think that your mind is weak. When their al in your world seeking you out, shut them down and close them out. Don't beg don't plead don't return the fight. Just hold you head up high and look to the sky and journey on with **your life**.

(POEM)

Shattered Dream

WHAT IS IT THAT YOU see when you look at me? Is it my smile my grin or my pretty teeth? What is it that you see when you look at me? It must be the glare in my eyes that hide the lies from the never ending lies and the silent cries. What is it that you see when you look at me? Can you feel the thunder does it make you wonder if I've fallen under and lost track of time and fallen behind from all the torment in the back of my mind? What is it that you see when you look at me? Do you notice the broken pieces or the thousand and one reasons that I'm crying on the inside from the pretty picture I was once painted of life? What is it that you see when you look at me? Is it the rainy days filled with clouds of haze that formed from the storms that once raged or can you clearly read what on the next page? What is it that you see when you look at me? Can you tell that my spirit is not well and I almost fell? What is it that you see when you're staring at me? Can you smell this awful potion that hides my emotions as I sit in silence while suffering from domestic violence? What is it that you see when you look at me? Do you notice the presence of the obsession that I have with life's lessons because I count them as blessings? What is it that you see when you look at me? Can you feel the breeze as I turn down the heat from the things that once intensified me? What is it that you see when you're looking at me? Are you asking yourself if you can get to know me or would you like to hold me and tell me you have better things you can show me? What is it that you see when you're looking at me? Are you trying to understand why I am who I am walking on dry land and how my story began? What is it that you see when you're looking at me? Does my character speak for itself or I have I placed it on a shelf with my confidence and common sense as I built a fence around my emptiness. What is it that you see when you're looking at me? Can you see the tears as I hide my fears that I've hid for years? What is it that you see when you look at me? Can you see the guilt behind this wall that I built or can you hear the sad song because they've done me so wrong? What is it that you see when you look at me? Can you see that God's still working on me as I'm trapped in insecurities? As tough as it seems I'm moving up stream as I pick up the pieces to my **Shattered Dream**.

A Reason Not to Cry

GIVE ME A REASON WHY I need to never say good bye give me a reason not to cry. Give me a peace of mind through the lonely days and restless nights. Give me a kiss on the cheek once in a while to let me know that everything will be alright. Give me a reason not to cry. I need the sun the moon the rivers and mountains, give me a water fountain. Give me someone who will pray when the times drifting away and tests and trials stand in my way. Give me a brighter day. Give me a tap on the shoulder as I start to get older and begin to wonder why my thoughts are taking me under. Give me shelter from the rain to ease the pain and comfort from the storm to keep me warm. Let me hear yes you can so I feel confident help me walk in my contentment. Give me someone to be there when I begin to fear give me someone to wipe my tears. Give me someone to hold me as my emotions control me. Give m a place to hide from the sunshine so I don't become blind. Give me a place to unwind. Give me someone to be true and to never lie. Give me someone who understands that love is life. Give me a partner in crime when the forces of evil attack my mind give me a ride or die. Give me a hug so tight in broad day light. Give me a reason not to cry. Give me a companion a true friend someone there through thick and thin someone to turn my frown to a grin. Give me a moment to erase the past from my cloudy mind give me some quality time.

Give me people so I'm never alone. Give me a place to call home. Give me rest and relaxation to get rid of this awful sensation that I wasn't born of this nation. I need a one on one relation because I'm one of God's creations. Give me a breath of life when my soul's slowly dying. **"Give me a thousand and one reasons to laugh to keep from crying."**

(POEM)

Now I Get It

If I'd knew back then what I know now, I would have been turned my life around, But my head was in the clouds when my feet touched the ground. Back then it never dawned on me that some people were wrong for me. Others were trying to protect me but I wouldn't listen so they just let me be. I didn't want them telling me what was best for me. The one' that would keep it real I didn't want them next to me. I told them to let me be and let me see what's behind door number one two and three. Being hurt do many times didn't teach me a lesson because I still fell for game lies and deception. So called friends I had not of them. I'm so glad I didn't fall for the next set of testing or I would have missed my blessing. Crying not denying that I did it but Gods grace and mercy kept me and **"Now I get it."**

A prayer For the Pure At Heart

LORD WALK WITH ME THROUGH this journey called life. Keep me on a path of straight and narrow. When my mind begins to wonder bring me back to a full focus. Let my light and my life be a guide to those who endure the same pain that I do. Cleanse my heart of all unclean spirits. Wake my spirit up to do the things necessary to please you. When I know no better grant me wisdom, knowledge and understanding. Hold back the things that are meant to destroy me and keep them far away. Surround me with people who will Love, Honor, cherish, encourage, and appreciate me for the human being that I am. Help me to hold tight to my integrity so my Godly character will speak for itself. Encamp a shield of protection around me and my loved ones the ones who care a great deal for me and realize that my life matters. Help me to teach others how to love themselves even when it seems as if no one else loves them. Supply me with all the tools I need to live a healthy prosperous live. Send me the Holy Spirit "a comforter" for those moments of despair. Wrap loving arms around me, when I feel like the world is on my shoulders and worry is weighing me down. Send sunshine when the rain storms begin to form puddles under my feet. Give me warning before destruction when I begin to travel the wrong roads. Show me signs of your wondrous works when I begin to believe I can do no better. When the odds are against me remind me that you are the Alpha and Omega the beginning and the end. Assure me that with you as my God no one or nothing can take away the things you bless me with. Allow my enemies to see you place me into higher heights in you. Make my enemies my foot stool. Pick me up when I begin to fall and strengthen me when I get weak. Ease the pain at those moments of disappointment and discouragement and show me how to still love those that hurt me. Restore my soul for your names sake. Lord these are the many blessings I ask in Your name I will give you all glory honor and praise at all times. Amen!!

Author Acknowledgements

I REALLY THANK GOD FOR walking me through this journey of writing a second book. I know that without Him I am nothing. If it was not for the wisdom and knowledge He provides me with I wouldn't have accomplished it. Writing a book to some may be easy but to others it is a process. I enjoy writing in my leisure time. I write about the things that are on my mind and in my heart. My writings are non fictional. I write about personal life experiences and try to recognize that other people go through the same things. I try to let readers know that there is always a way out of every situation.

I would like to thank the ones who are always there for me and who really believe in me and have my back one hundred percent. There's too many of them to name them all. They know who they are. I have to extend a special thank you to those that pushed me to be a better me. I would like to thank Angela Lewis who is a great mentor and life coach a person who encourages people to believe in their dreams. I would like to thank Japera Henderson who keeps pushing and encouraging me to go a step further in what I do. I would like to thank My middle Daughter Asia king who holds a very special place in my heart she gave me the idea for my book cover and my Sister in Law Chrishana Dixon who helped design it. My other two daughters Nyjira Dixon and Tanaya King who inspire me daily. Love to All!!!

Printed in the United States
By Bookmasters